DISCOVERING THE UNITED STATES

Nevada

BY ANGELA LIM

Kids Core
An Imprint of Abdo Publishing
abdobooks.com

abdobooks.com

Published by Abdo Publishing, a division of ABDO, PO Box 398166, Minneapolis, Minnesota 55439.

Printed in China.
052024
092024

Cover Photo: iStockphoto
Interior Photos: Shutterstock Images, 4–5, 17, 26; Double Brow Imagery/Shutterstock Images, 6 (top left); Dominic Gentilcore/Shutterstock Images, 6 (top right); iStockphoto, 6 (bottom left), 15, 28 (top right); Will Pedro/Shutterstock Images, 6 (bottom right); BlickWinkel/Baesemann/Alamy, 9; Kit Leong/Shutterstock Images, 10; David Cobb/Alamy, 12–13; Sean M. Haffey/Getty Images Sport/Getty Images, 16; Cavan Images/iStockphoto, 19; Jacob Boomsma/Shutterstock Images, 20–21; Sean Pavone/Shutterstock Images, 22; William Cushman/Shutterstock Images, 23; Joseph Sohm/Shutterstock Images, 25; Red Line Editorial, 28 (top left), 29; Neil Lockhart/Shutterstock Images, 28 (bottom left); Claudio Del Luongo/Shutterstock Images, 28 (bottom right)

Editor: Christa Kelly
Series Designer: Katharine Hale

Library of Congress Control Number: 2023949358

Publisher's Cataloging-in-Publication Data

Names: Lim, Angela, author.
Title: Nevada / by Angela Lim
Description: Minneapolis, Minnesota: Abdo Publishing, 2025 | Series: Discovering the United States | Includes online resources and index.
Identifiers: ISBN 9781098293987 (lib. bdg.) | ISBN 9798384913252 (ebook)
Subjects: LCSH: U.S. states--Juvenile literature. | Nevada--History--Juvenile literature. | Western States (U.S.)--Juvenile literature. | Physical geography--United States--Juvenile literature.
Classification: DDC 973--dc23

All population data taken from:
"Estimates of Population by Sex, Race, and Hispanic Origin: April 1, 2020 to July 1, 2022." *US Census Bureau, Population Division,* June 2023, census.gov.

CONTENTS

The amount of concrete used to build the Hoover Dam could pave a road from California to New York.

CHAPTER 1

The Hoover Dam

It was March 1, 1936. The Hoover Dam was finally finished. It had taken five years to build. The dam was named after Herbert Hoover. He had been president when construction began.

The dam spanned the Colorado River in Nevada.

Nevada Facts

DATE OF STATEHOOD
October 31, 1864

CAPITAL
Carson City

POPULATION
3,177,772

AREA
110,572 square miles
(286,380 sq km)

STATE BIRD

Mountain bluebird

STATE TREE ONE

Single-leaf piñon

STATE FLOWER

Sagebrush

STATE TREE TWO

Bristlecone pine

Each US state has a different population, size, and capital city. States also have state symbols.

It controlled the flow of the river. It created a **reservoir**. The Hoover Dam would provide water to people living in the desert-filled region.

A big celebration was held when the Hoover Dam was finished. About 20,000 people came to the dam on its opening day. President Franklin D. Roosevelt was among them. He gave a speech.

Onlookers stood on the road at the top of the structure. Beneath them, tons of smooth concrete held back the mighty Colorado River. The visitors looked down in wonder at the tallest dam in the world.

Nevada's Land

Nevada is in the West region of the United States. Idaho and Oregon form the state's northern border. Utah lies to the east.

Arizona borders Nevada to the southeast. California is to the west and southwest.

Most of Nevada is desert. Rock formations called **mesas** are scattered throughout the state. Though Nevada is mostly dry, the state has a few large natural lakes. These include Pyramid Lake and Lake Tahoe. Nevada also has mountains and valleys.

Nevada's Desert Plants

Nevada is very dry. But plants still grow. Many types of wildflowers bloom in Nevada's deserts in the spring. Cacti and shrubs also grow. These plants can survive with little water.

Mormon Mesa formed up to 5 million years ago.

Nevada has more than 300 mountain ranges.

Climate

Nevada is the driest state in the United States. It receives only 9.5 inches (24 cm) of rainfall each year. But some mountainous parts of the state get heavy snow.

Temperatures vary across the state. Northern Nevada gets very cold during the winter. Southern Nevada is hot for most of the year.

Explore Online

Visit the website below. What new information did you learn about Nevada that wasn't in Chapter One?

Nevada

abdocorelibrary.com/discovering-nevada

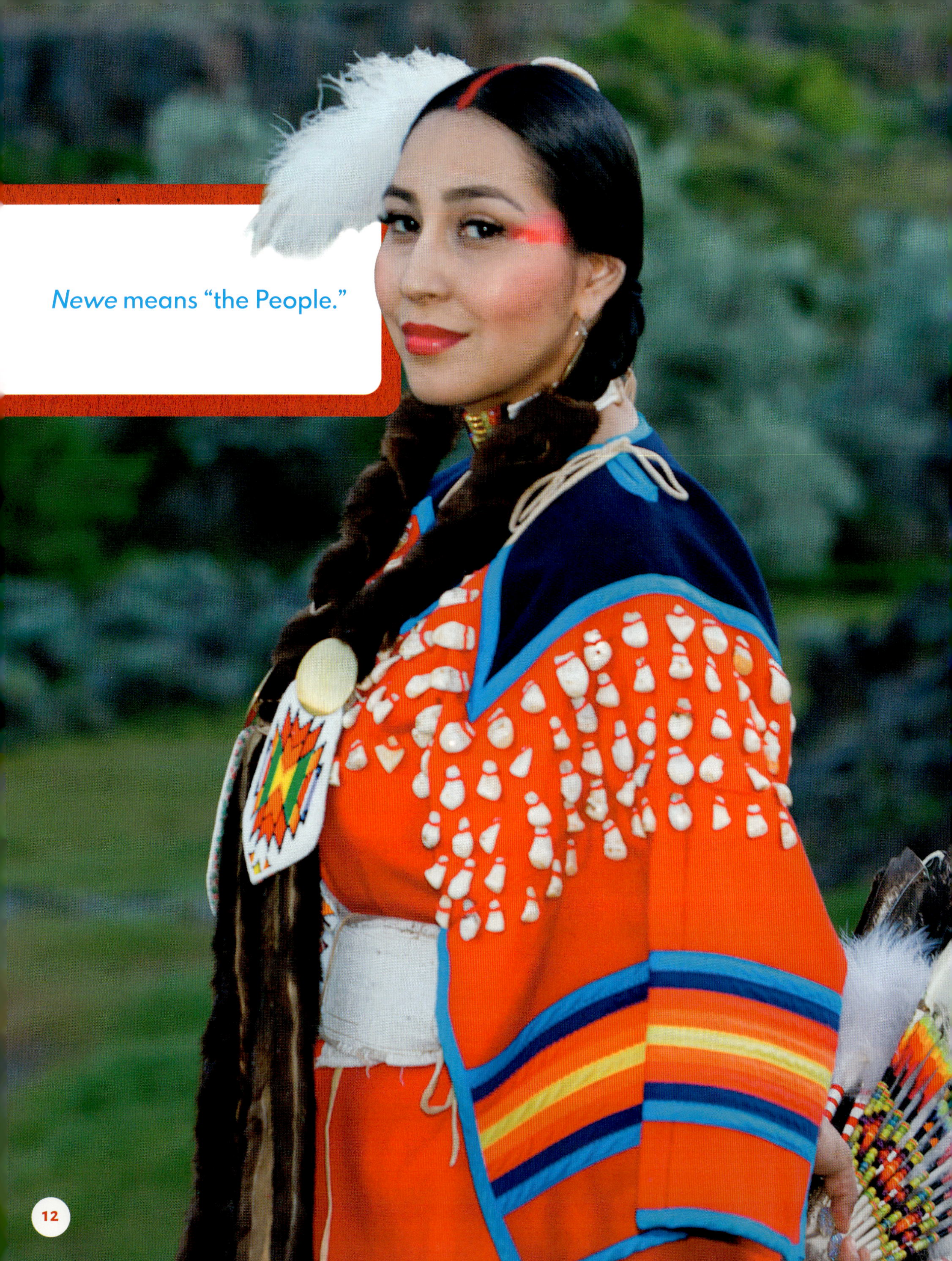

Newe means "the People."

CHAPTER 2

The People of Nevada

People have lived in Nevada for 20,000 years. The first people in the region were American Indians. They formed nations. These include the Newe (or Shoshone), Wašiw (or Washoe), Northern Paiute, Southern Paiute, and Hualapai nations.

Today, Nevada is home to 28 federally recognized American Indian nations.

Spanish explorers arrived in the 1770s. They named the area *Nevada*. This means "snow covered." The Spanish chose the name due to the snow-capped mountain peaks.

Silver and gold were discovered in Nevada in the 1850s. These resources brought many white **settlers** to the region. They stole land from American Indians. The booming population led Nevada to become a state in 1864.

Today, almost 46 percent of Nevada's population is white. About 30 percent is Hispanic or Latino. Almost 11 percent is Black. A little more than 9 percent is Asian, and nearly

The silver star on Nevada's flag represents the silver found in the state.

2 percent is American Indian. Almost 1 percent is Native Hawaiian and Pacific Islander.

Culture

Food is an important part of Nevada's culture. In the fall, people in Nevada hunt elk. The meat is used in many meals, including elk chops.

The Raiders originally played for California before moving to Las Vegas in 2020.

Fry bread tacos are also popular. So is shrimp cocktail. This is a platter of shrimp with sauce.

Sports are also important in Nevada. The state has seven professional sports teams. The Las Vegas Raiders are among the most popular. They play in the National Football League (NFL). The Las Vegas Aces are another popular team. They are part of the Women's National Basketball Association (WNBA).

Nevada has many unique attractions. The Sphere is an entertainment arena with a giant 360-degree video screen.

Industries

Tourism is one of Nevada's most important **industries**. Gambling was made legal across the state in 1931. Gambling is an activity where people try to win money in games of luck and skill. Today, Nevada has more than 200 **casinos**. They attract many visitors.

People also travel to Nevada for live entertainment. The state holds many concerts and magic shows.

Mining is another important industry in Nevada. Gold, silver, and copper are mined in the state. Nevada is also the only US state with lithium mines. This **mineral** is used in electronic devices. In 2022, Nevada's mineral

Area 51

The US military has several bases in Nevada. Area 51 is among the most famous. It is in southern Nevada. The US Air Force uses the base for flight testing. Most of the activities in Area 51 are top secret. Some people think the base is secretly used to research alien spacecraft. But there is no proof to support this claim.

Some people say lithium mining harms the environment and threatens American Indian historical sites.

production was worth nearly $9 billion. The state ranked second in the country behind Arizona.

Further Evidence

Look at the website below. Does it give any new evidence to support Chapter Two?

American Indians of Nevada

abdocorelibrary.com/discovering-nevada

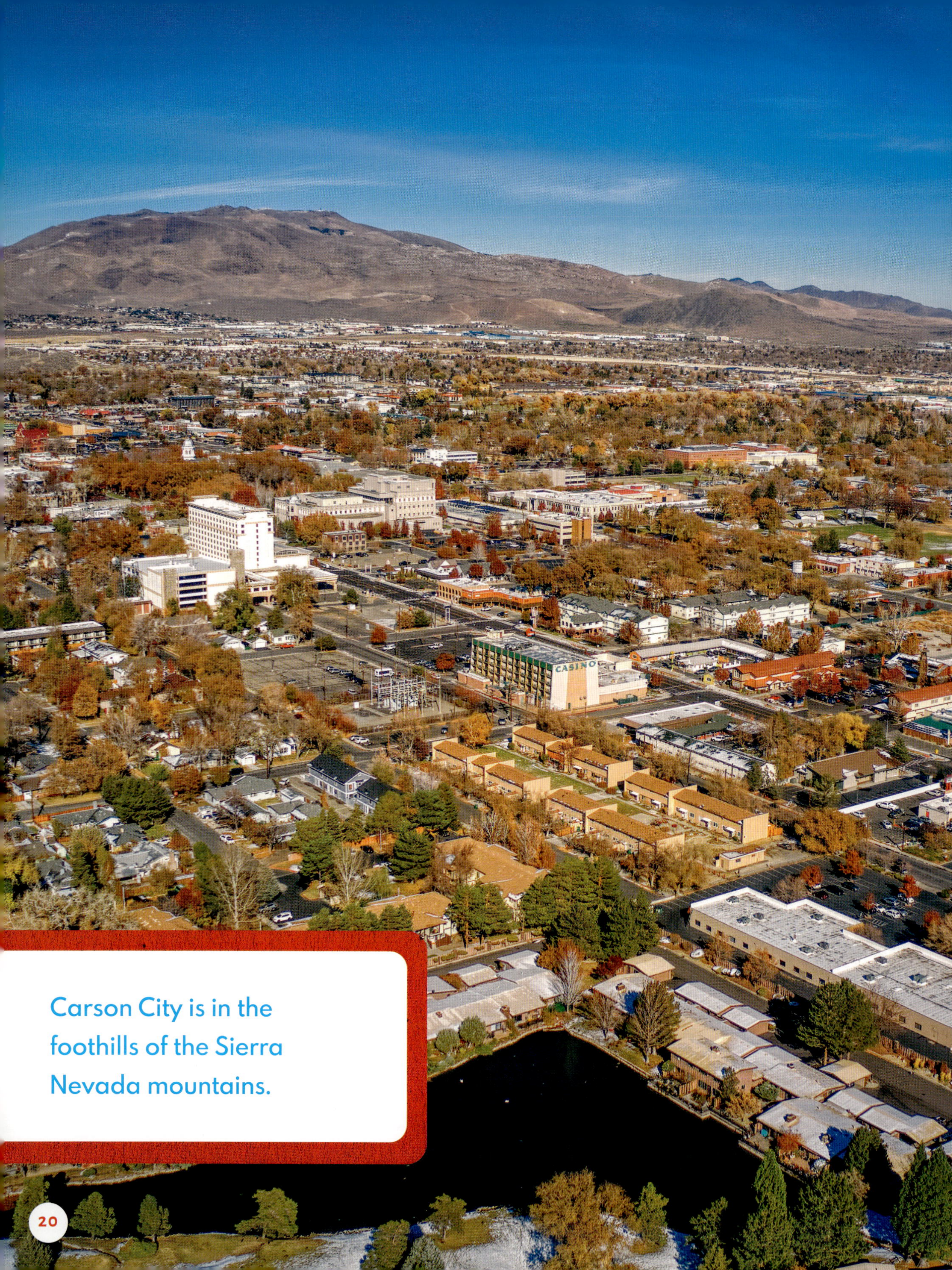

Carson City is in the foothills of the Sierra Nevada mountains.

Places in Nevada

Carson City is the capital of Nevada. Visitors can learn about the state's history at the Nevada State Museum. They can learn about trains at the Nevada State Railroad Museum.

Las Vegas is the most **populated** city in Nevada.

Las Vegas's famous welcome sign was built in 1959.

It is home to more than 650,000 people. Many more people visit every year. In 2022, the city saw more than 38 million visitors.

Las Vegas is packed with hotels and casinos. It also has more than 500 restaurants. Tourists can also enjoy the city's amusement parks, aquariums, and live entertainment.

Slow-moving slabs of ice called glaciers formed the land in Great Basin National Park 10,000 years ago.

Parks

Nevada has two national parks. Great Basin National Park protects bristlecone pine **groves**. These trees are among the oldest trees on Earth. They can live for more than 4,000 years. The park is also home to Wheeler Peak, one of the highest points in Nevada. Visitors come to the park to hike, stargaze, and tour the park's caves.

Death Valley National Park is shared between Nevada and California. The park covers 3.4 million acres (1.4 million ha). About 110,000 acres (44,500 ha) of this land is in Nevada. The park is the hottest and driest place in the United States. It is famous for its desert landscapes.

Ghost Towns

Many people came to Nevada in the 1860s when silver was discovered. Towns sprang up throughout the state. But many were abandoned when the silver began to run out. The abandoned towns are now called ghost towns. Today, Nevada has more than 600 ghost towns that people can visit.

Fort Churchill's buildings are made of adobe, which is a mixture of sand, clay, and water.

Landmarks

One of Nevada's most famous landmarks is the Fort Churchill State Historic Park. The park is in the western part of the state. The fort was built in 1860. It was the first US military post in the region. The fort protected early settlers. It was abandoned just nine years later. Today, visitors can tour the ruins and visitor center. They can also camp and hike in the park.

Lake Tahoe is more than 2 million years old.

Lake Tahoe is on the border of California and Nevada. It is the second-deepest lake in the country. It is also the clearest lake in the country. In some areas, people can see more than 70 feet (21 m) down into the lake.

Nevada is a fascinating state. It has entertainment, history, and natural beauty. The state is full of amazing places to explore.

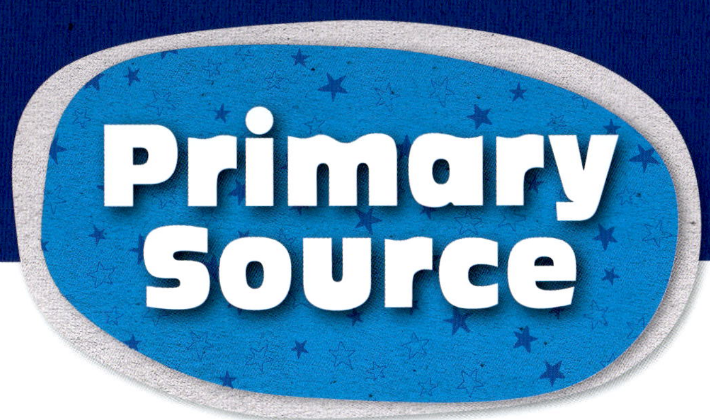

Bradley Mills is a ranger at Great Basin National Park. He says:

> On a really, really good night, you can see thousands and thousands of stars. In the summertime, the Milky Way is just stretching right above your head.

Source: Eve Chen. "'A Little Oasis': What Travelers Are Missing by Skipping Great Basin National Park." *USA Today*, 7 Oct. 2023, usatoday.com. Accessed 16 Nov. 2023.

Comparing Texts

Think about the quote. Does it support the information in this chapter? Or does it give a different perspective? Explain how in a few sentences.

State Map

KEY

Capital

Park

City or town

Point of interest

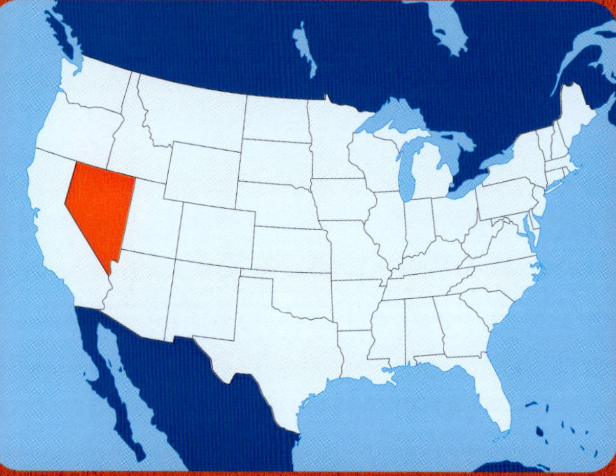

Colorado River

Death Valley National Park

Pyramid Lake

Nevada: The Silver State

Glossary

casinos
public places where people play gambling games

groves
small groups of trees

industry
a group of businesses that serve similar purposes

mesas
hills with flat tops, often found in deserts

mineral
a substance formed in the earth that is not of an animal or a plant

populated
settled or lived in

reservoir
a human-made lake that is typically used as a water supply

settlers
people who moved to a new area

Online Resources

To learn more about Nevada, visit our free resource websites below.

Visit **abdocorelibrary.com** or scan this QR code for free Common Core resources for teachers and students, including vetted activities, multimedia, and booklinks, for deeper subject comprehension.

Visit **abdobooklinks.com** or scan this QR code for free additional online weblinks for further learning. These links are routinely monitored and updated to provide the most current information available.

Learn More

Murray, Julie. *Nevada.* Abdo, 2020.

Payne, Stefanie. *The National Parks.* DK, 2020.

Wyner, Zach and John Willis. *Las Vegas Raiders.* AV2, 2021.

Index

About the Author

Angela Lim is an MFA student in poetry at Indiana University in Bloomington, Indiana.